MAP BASICS

All About

PHYSICAL MAPS

By Barbara M. Linde

Gareth Stevens PUBLISHING

Please visit our website, www.garethstevens.com. For a free color catalog of all our high-quality books, call toll free 1-800-542-2595 or fax 1-877-542-2596.

Cataloging-in-Publishing Data

Names: Linde, Barbara M.
Title: All about physical maps / Barbara M. Linde.
Description: New York : Gareth Stevens Publishing, 2019. | Series: Map basics | Includes glossary and index.
Identifiers: ISBN 9781538232620 (pbk.) | ISBN 9781538229163 (library bound) | ISBN 9781538232637 (6pack)
Subjects: LCSH: Maps–Juvenile literature. | Topographic maps–Juvenile literature.
Classification: LCC GA105.6 L686 2019 | DDC 912–dc23

Published in 2019 by
Gareth Stevens Publishing
111 East 14th Street, Suite 349
New York, NY 10003

Designer: Sarah Liddell
Editor: Monika Davies

Photo credits: Cover, p. 1 Cartarium/Shutterstock.com; pp. 5, 9 Bardocz Peter/Shutterstock.com; p. 7 AridOcean/Shutterstock.com; p. 11 Planet Observer/UIG/Universal Images Group/Getty Images; p. 13 Volodymyr Nikulishyn/Shutterstock.com; p. 15 Schwabenblitz/Shutterstock.com; p. 17 Buyenlarge/ Contributor/Archive Photos/Getty Images; p. 19 NASA/GSFC/Arizona State University/Cocu/ Wikimedia Commons; p. 20 Sawitree Pamee/EyeEm/EyeEm/Getty Images.

Printed in the United States of America

CPSIA compliance information: Batch #CW19GS: For further information contact Gareth Stevens, New York, New York at 1-800-542-2595.

CONTENTS

Words in the glossary appear in **bold** type the first time they are used in the text.

WHAT IS A PHYSICAL MAP?

Suppose you want to take a trip. You want to be in the mountains, near a lake, and far away from a desert. How can you find the perfect place? One way is to use a physical map. This kind of map helps you learn what an area of land looks like.

Physical maps show the land's natural features, which are called landforms. Mountains, hills, forests, and deserts are all landforms. Physical maps also show bodies of water, such as oceans, rivers, and lakes.

JUST THE FACTS

Physical maps are also called landform maps.

PHYSICAL MAP OF ASIA

This physical map shows landforms in Asia, one of the world's seven **continents**.

COLORS ARE IMPORTANT!

Colors give important clues about the landforms on a map. The color blue usually stands for water. A blue line, for example, often represents a river. The color green usually marks where plants or trees are growing.

The relief, or how high or low something is, may be shown in shades of brown—from light for low to dark for high. The **legend** on the map explains what the different colors mean.

JUST THE FACTS

Physical maps can also include **political** borders and capital cities.

RELIEF MAP OF ALASKA

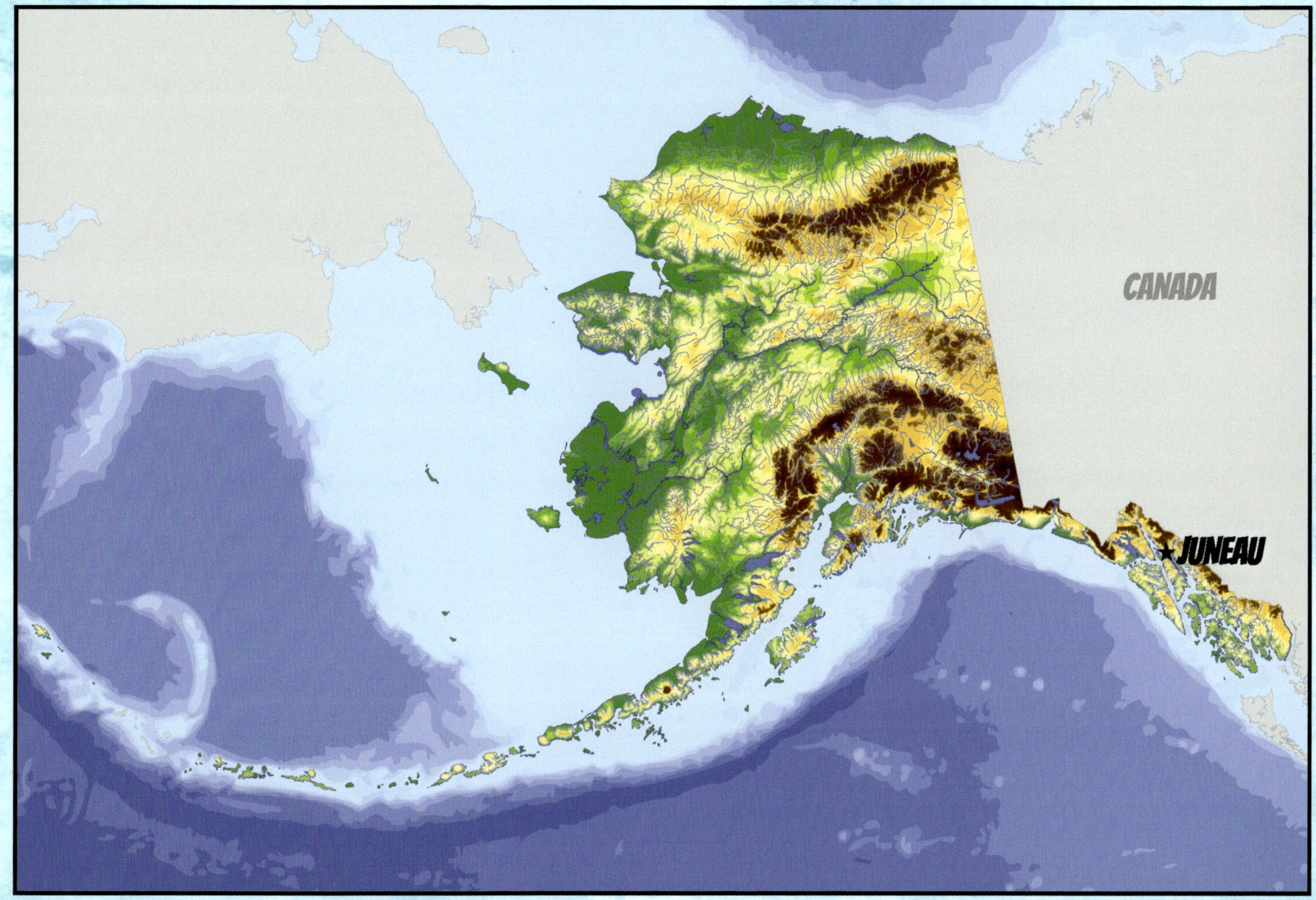

On this map of Alaska, the highest mountains are dark brown, while the lowest areas are shaded dark green.

THE COMPASS ROSE

Somewhere on a map, you'll see a compass rose. A compass rose helps you tell directions when you're looking at a map. The cardinal, or main, directions are north, south, east, and west.

This is a map of North America. Using the compass rose, you can see that the Rocky Mountains run through western Canada down into New Mexico in the United States. Five large lakes, known as the Great Lakes, are found in eastern North America along the border between the United States and Canada.

JUST THE FACTS

The compass rose was first put on maps around the 1300s.

The Gulf of Mexico, a large body of water that connects to the Atlantic Ocean, is south of the United States and east of Mexico.

USING THE SCALE

Near the bottom of most maps, you'll see something that looks like a small ruler. This is called a scale. Maps show areas of land much smaller than they are in real life. A scale uses smaller distances to represent larger distances. For example, 1 inch (2.5 cm) on the map might equal 1 mile (1.6 km) in real life. The scale will give you more information about distances.

The Appalachian Trail is around 2,200 miles (3,541 km) long. How many miles of the trail run through Pennsylvania?

JUST THE FACTS

No cars or other **vehicles** are allowed on the Appalachian Trail. It's the longest trail in the world made just for hiking.

On the map, about 2 inches (5 cm) of the Appalachian Trail run through Pennsylvania. Using the scale, you can figure out that this equals a little over 200 miles (322 km) in real life.

COMPARING CONTINENTS

This physical map shows the continents of Europe, Asia, Africa, and Australia. These are four of Earth's seven great landmasses. Asia is the largest continent, while Australia is the smallest.

You can use a map to compare landforms on each continent. For example, this physical map shows that Africa and parts of Asia have large deserts. Australia's desert is smaller. Each continent on this map has some grasslands, too.

JUST THE FACTS

The Sahara in northern Africa is the largest hot desert on Earth. It's 3.5 million square miles (9,064,958 sq km)!

WORLD LANDFORMS

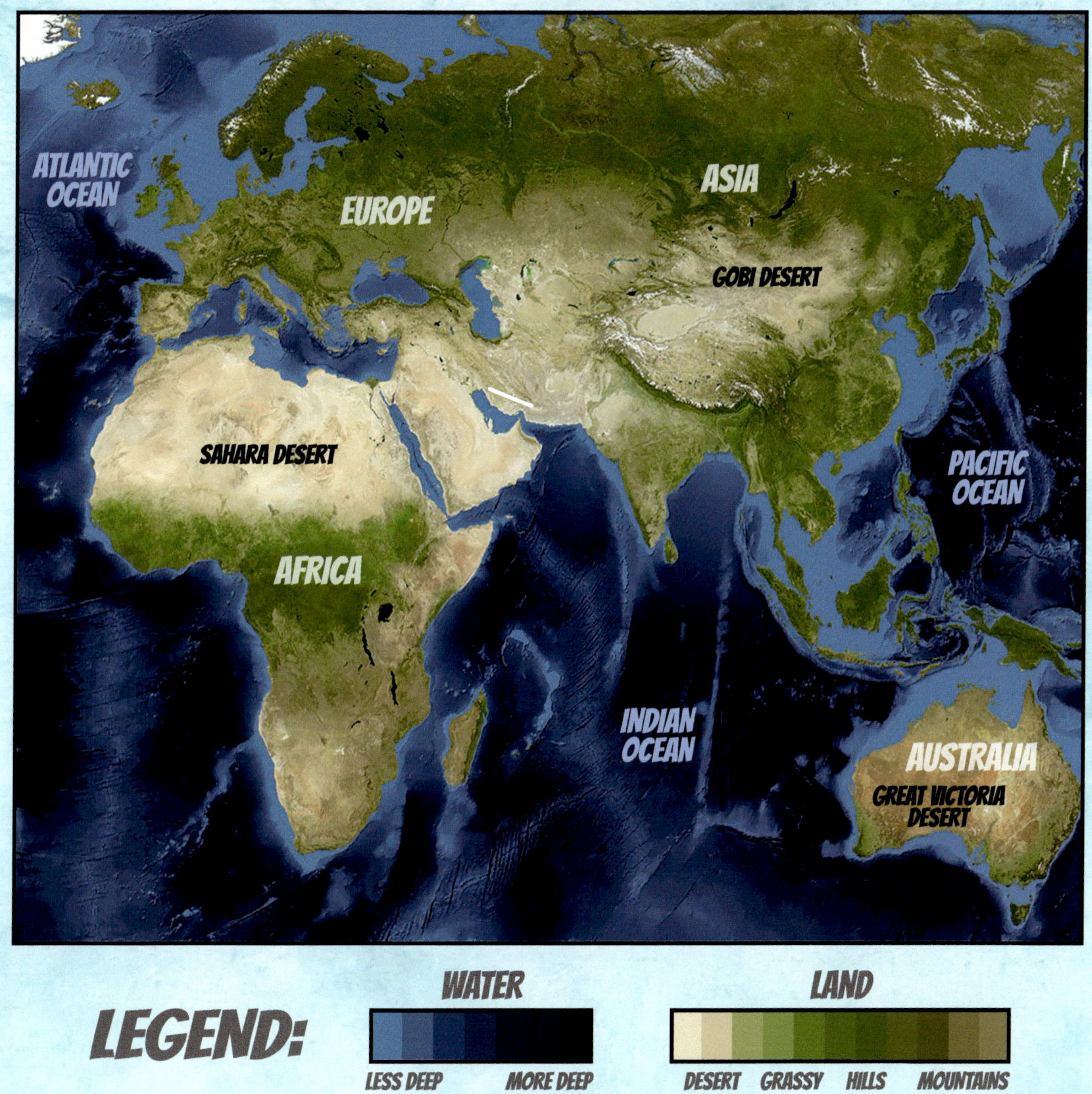

"Sahara" means "desert" in the language of Arabic.

A MAP FOR ONE PURPOSE

Sometimes physical maps highlight, or call out, an important feature of the land. This map, for example, shows the Colorado River **Aqueduct**, which provides Southern California with more than half of its water supply.

The aqueduct starts along the border of Arizona and California at the Parker Dam on the Colorado River. It then flows west. On the map, the darker blue line representing the aqueduct ends at the city of Los Angeles, California, which is on a flat plain.

JUST THE FACTS

The Colorado River Aqueduct is 242 miles (389.5 km) long.

This map also shows the **boundary** lines between California, Arizona, and Nevada, as well as California and Baja California, which is part of Mexico.

COLORADO RIVER AQUEDUCT

THE OCEAN FLOOR

If you head to the beach and walk into the ocean, you might think the ocean floor is completely flat. However, like Earth's surface, the ocean floor has mountains, valleys, and other landforms.

Scientists use special tools to map the features of the ocean floor, such as the Mid-Atlantic Ridge and the Mariana **Trench**. At about 10,000 miles (16,093 km) long, the Mid-Atlantic Ridge is the world's longest mountain range! The Mariana Trench is the deepest point on Earth at more than 36,000 feet (10,973 m).

JUST THE FACTS

The Mariana Trench is over 1,580 miles (2,543 km) long and around 43 miles (69 km) wide.

On this map, darker blue shading shows the mountain ranges on the ocean floor. Areas of lighter blue show parts of the ocean floor that are flat or less mountainous.

THE OCEAN FLOOR AND THE MARIANA TRENCH

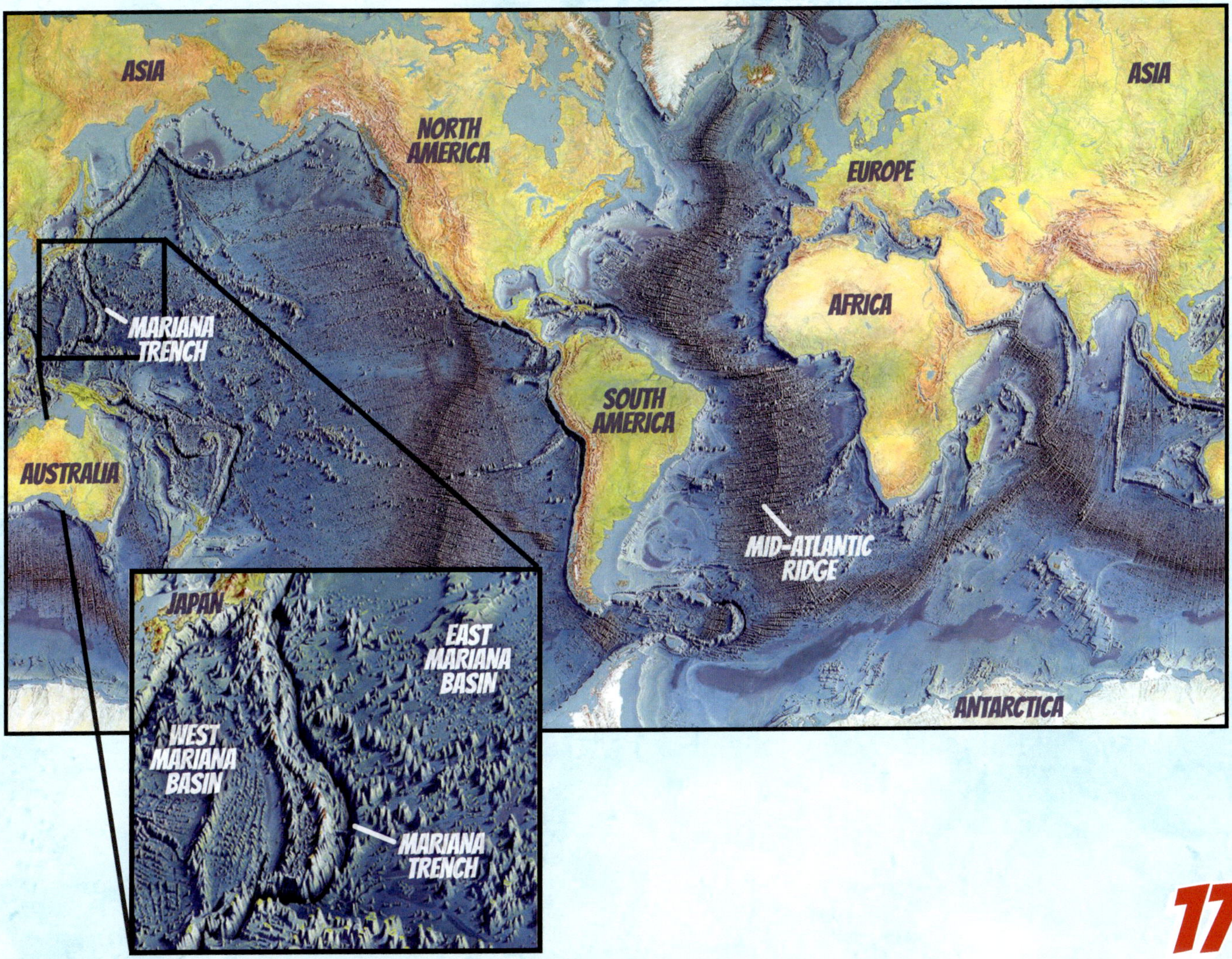

OUT OF THIS WORLD MAPS

Did you know that NASA (National Aeronautics and Space Administration) creates maps of moons and planets in space? Spacecraft orbit a moon or planet, while special tools on board take measurements and pictures. These facts and figures are then sent back to Earth, where scientists use the information to make physical maps.

This is a physical map of the surface of Earth's moon. Each dark spot, called a mare, is a large basin, or bowl-shaped dip, on the moon's surface.

JUST THE FACTS

In 1609, Thomas Harriot made the first map of the moon by looking at it through a **telescope**.

Craters are large holes on the moon's surface. They form when objects in space **collide** with the moon. Plato, Copernicus, and Ptolemaeus are craters.

THE SURFACE OF THE MOON

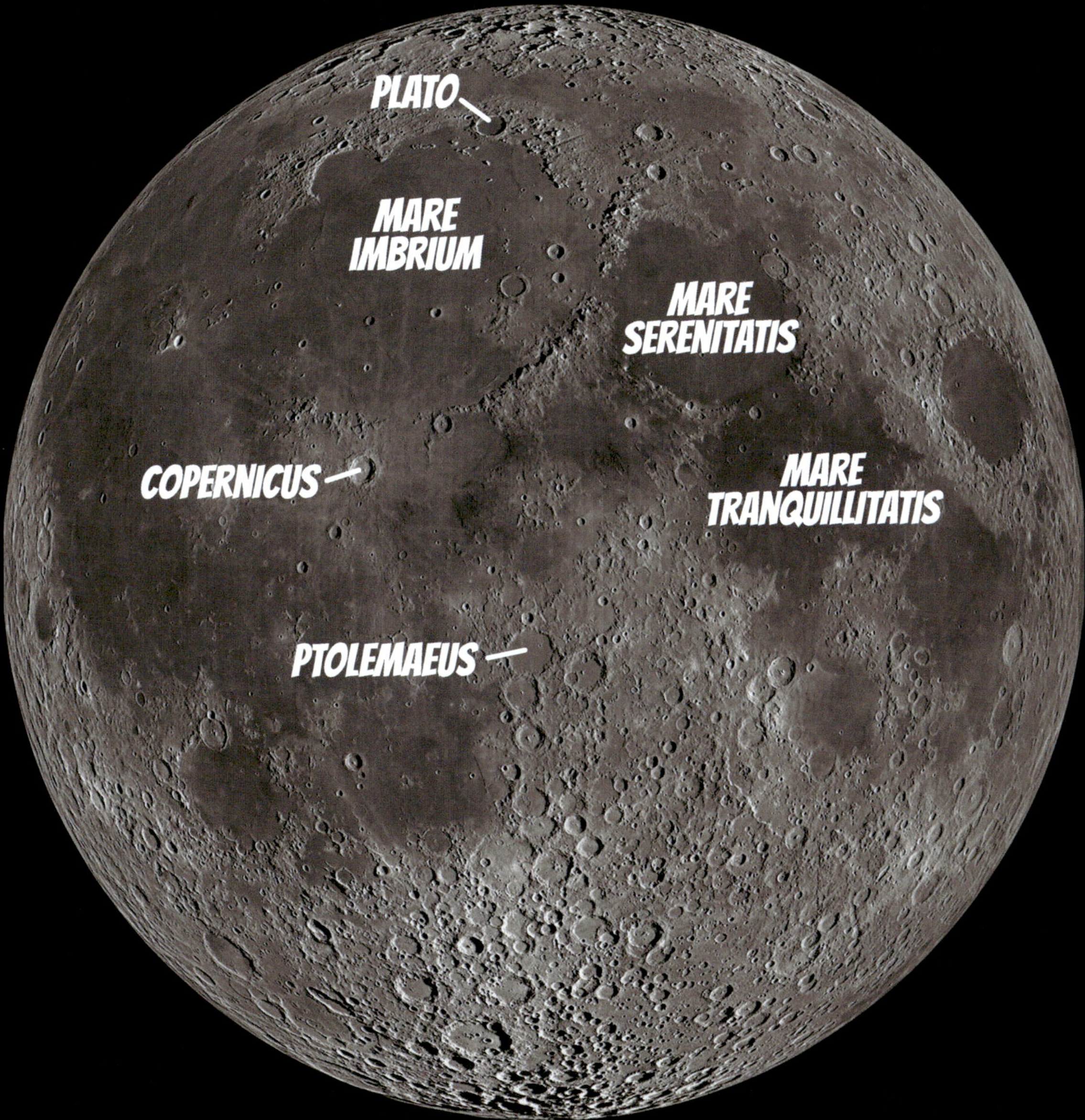

MAP IT!

What kind of places do you like to visit? Do you like traveling to places with lots of mountains? Or, do you like going to places that are very flat? Or, perhaps you like going to areas near the water!

Draw a physical map of an imaginary place you'd like to visit. Then, show your map to your classmates, and ask them if they can understand your map. If they can't, make changes to your map so it's easier to understand.

MAKE YOUR OWN PHYSICAL MAP!

1. FIND A LARGE SHEET OF PAPER AND A FEW CRAYONS OR COLORED PENCILS.
2. MAKE UP A NAME FOR THE PLACE YOU'D LIKE TO VISIT AND WRITE IT AT THE TOP OF THE PAPER.
3. DOES THIS PLACE HAVE BODIES OF WATER, MOUNTAINS, OR FLAT AREAS? DRAW THE DIFFERENT LANDFORMS ON YOUR SHEET OF PAPER.
4. GIVE EACH LANDFORM A NAME. THEN, COLOR IN THE LAND'S RELIEF.
5. ADD A LEGEND THAT EXPLAINS WHAT THE DIFFERENT COLORS ON YOUR PHYSICAL MAP MEAN.
6. DON'T FORGET TO INCLUDE A COMPASS ROSE ON YOUR PHYSICAL MAP!

GLOSSARY

aqueduct: a man-made channel used to carry water from one place to another

boundary: something (such as a river, a fence, or an imaginary line) that shows where one area ends and another area begins

collide: the hitting of two objects against one another

continent: one of Earth's seven great landmasses

legend: a list or diagram that explains the colors or pictures used on a map

political: having to do with the activities of the government and government officials

telescope: a tool that makes faraway objects look bigger and closer

trench: a long, thin, deep channel in the ocean floor

vehicle: an object used for moving people or goods, such as a car, truck, or airplane

FOR MORE INFORMATION

BOOKS

National Geographic Society. *National Geographic Kids United States Atlas*. Washington, DC: National Geographic, 2017.

Rand McNally. *World Atlas: Grades 1–3*. Skokie, IL: Rand McNally, 2018.

Rice, William B. *Landforms*. Huntington Beach, CA: Teacher Created Materials, 2015.

WEBSITES

Continents
www.dkfindout.com/uk/earth/continents
Discover the seven continents of the world, and learn which mountains, rivers, and deserts are located on each continent.

Landforms
www.edu.pe.ca/southernkings/landforms.htm
Find out more about mountains, hills, glaciers, and other landforms shown on a physical map.

MapMaker Interactive
mapmaker.nationalgeographic.org
Explore the world using National Geographic's interactive map program.

INDEX